The Sea Lion
Who
Saved the Boy
Who
Jumped from the Golden Gate

The Sea Lion
Who
Saved the Boy
Who
Jumped from the Golden Gate

Jane McCafferty

Saddle Road Press

Saddle Road Press
Ithaca, New York
saddleroadpress.com

Book design by Don Mitchell
California Sea Lion photograph by Andrea Izzotti (iStock)

ISBN 9798987954119
Library of Congress Control Number: 2023939722

Books by Jane McCafferty

Director of the World and other stories
One Heart
Thank You For the Music
First You Try Everything

For Gibbons Ruark

I am the least difficult of men. All I want is boundless love.

—Frank O'Hara

Contents

I

I

Do You Speak Hafez?

It was the year we conceded we'd be in recovery
for the rest of our lives. We dressed like twins in coats

of quivering blackbirds. Their furious heartbeats
warmed our skin — we thought this might be enough.

The poet Hafez whispered in your ear: "It is not possible
to complete yourself without sorrow."

Later one by one the birds took off with pieces
of our faith in their beaks. You could see the bare patches

of our flesh like islands. Then they all were gone,
and the sky was their new home, so many birds above us

singing as we walked naked, subsumed by fear.
And Hafez whispered in my ear:

"All your problems can be solved — just untie the sun
that somehow got leashed on a pole inside you."

Do you speak Hafez, you said, and I who took Hafez
to bed at night said yes, I speak Hafez, I try to speak Hafez.

And you said long live Hafez whose heart is always dying
to get close to the Mercy, may we pass it on to the imprisoned.

May we pass it on and on when darkness comes.

THE LIST

I had a notion to put a small bronze horse in my pocket.
I had a notion to wash the pears and set them on the ledge to glow.
I had a notion to hold that old man's hand on the bus.
Notions follow me like invisible birds, pecking my neck.

I had a notion to paint a dove on each brick of my house.
I had a notion to choose the shelter's homeliest dog.
I spent a day imagining I could not continue.
What a notion that was.

I had a notion to sing *If I could be who you wanted*
and another to worship basil.
I had a notion to sweep the streets clean in the dawn.
I have the everyday notion to toss my thoughts into the violet flame.

I miss my children every day and have a notion not to say it.
Others have lost children to war, to death, to hatreds.
When you swim through darkness, try calling it velvet.
When you ache, try calling it living.
I have a notion everyone I meet out there is the one for me.
I have a notion to blame my life on A.D.H.D.

I have a notion that everything that happened is still happening,
My children still run through the sprinkler,
their laughter like chimes in the light.

Something happened to my back.
I've not been able to walk myself into blistering light.
My gratitude tries escaping like Vasko Popa's mangled wolf.

Great joy abounds on earth, and we get glimpses.
I have a notion to thank you, to love you, for being here.

TREE SHADOWS

On the white sun-struck wall of Home Depot
three of them shivered like they knew
I was falling for them.
The littler one might have broken into something
like a tree dance had I more time and vision.

They were ordinary trees but of course
there is no such thing — the way they can't help
reaching — so unlike us. The way
they seem happily resigned to their form,
their dependence on slow growth.

It's hard to say anything new about trees.

I like those pictures of old women living
in tree-houses, their wild hair hanging down.
I always listen hard when people say old women
should cut their hair, and wonder why.
I remember my mother saying so and so
is too old for all that hair. Back then too old
was forty, fifty at most.

I can't say I'm looking forward
to being old. Being almost old
is where I'd like to stay. Here on this cliff,
not yet a stranger in the mirror,
but the aches starting up
like an interesting orchestra I ignore.

Am I saying aging is a kind
of music and expecting you to believe it?
I can't remember the last tree I climbed.
I was probably a long-haired child hanging
upside down, lapping up the sky and yelling
Hey You! to passers-by,
just showing off, not caring that my shirt

17

was probably up around my head.
I guess I won't be doing that again.

Unless I turn into one of those wild bird-women
far beyond the eyes of others.

Out Walking

"A chair in the snow is always sad."
—Jane Hirshfield

But I saw one that was happy, Jane.
It was so happy to be sitting there on the curb
it was almost laughing. The interior life

of the green cushions burst in the night
like golden blossoms. The snow came down like bullets,
but the blossoms softly received what fell.

Jane, the snow settled on the green arms
like grandmother's lace. I know the people
who put the chair out on the curb, sort of,

or rather I spy through their beautiful lit window
when I'm out here alone. I know we all love lit windows
in the houses of strangers but why do they make us ache

until we want to walk in the front door
and become other people so we can take a seat
at the stranger's table, say "Have you seen that chair

out there? It's not sad." And enjoy the macaroni and cheese,
the red wine, any talk that doesn't touch on the governing forces.
I know two people who think this is their last earthly incarnation.

They don't share my lust for the lives of strangers
framed in lit windows. They are smarter, maybe,
and just want into a realm without suffering.

I guess in certain moods I feel the same, but tonight,
falling in love with a stuffed green chair in the snow,
looking into two lit windows where families gather

in the blue light of television, I want to stay here forever,
until my spirit knows how to reside in a thousand different bodies,
a thousand neighborhoods, a million chairs, waiting in the snow.

VLADIMIR, PLEASE

I decided today I'll not be afraid
like someone dodging an executioner

who is always stealthily approaching
with a loud declaration of my mistakes,

crashing cymbals in the air beside
my head, poking me in the chest—

and this has nothing to do with Vladimir
throwing another tantrum, though I wish

I could blame him. And yet maybe I can
since we all know there's no such thing

as separation anymore. We are one
giant organism dreaming a nightmare.

Today I'll walk down slippery streets
like my shoes are popular, like I'm really

from here, a person who understands the customs,
someone who stops on the corner,

waiting for red to turn to emerald green,
part of the small crowd crossing in deep winds,

following the woman in her forsythia-yellow headscarf
and dark gold coat who I need to forgive

for not being my mother, for not turning to me
and noticing my unreasonable forsakenness,

my desire for embrace, to sit head to head in the grief
of a dark place that reeks of cinnamon

or Turkish coffee and bread, talking
not of loneliness but of Mr. Putin with his finger

trembling near the button and how they're calling
crimes against humanity on these Russians

as if we haven't been droning for decades,
propping up dictators like blind dolls on a bed.

I don't remember when I stopped feeling
somebody will save us, somebody will

turn the ship from the abyss
and there she goes—

the yellow scarf and golden coat into the grey
tunnel of the sky, the sky I'm photographing

every day of my life, the sky which is another name
for the heart I want to give you

now, with all these clouds.
Please Vladimir, don't be as crazy evil

as I fear you are, please just eat some circus peanuts,
throw them into the air and catch them with your mouth

to impress a grandchild who might sit in a sauna
with you later, whispering don't destroy the world,

a kid who opens the door to the sauna because
he still loves watching the snow fall

Bolivian Orphanage

Gringo, the two year old orphans
 clutch your legs, still wanting
            to be lifted
            to be held

here in this room where they bang
their heads hard on the walls as if
to the beat of an old brute song,

song of left-on-the steps, song
of always hungry, song being blasted
in and out of the core of this earth.

You try to entertain, hold
            a stuffed dog high in the air,
give him a cartoon voice, jump back
            when he barks. Some stare
uncomprehending, but one small child
            does a wild dance, black eyes shining,
his laughter rising,
      encircling you.

A girl you carry can't stop
            crying, eyes
            accusing you,
face contorted with rage.
            What does she need you to do?
Right now.

The world is balancing on their backs,
said Padre Juancho.

You'll grow old hoping
one of them will save you.

THE 1980's

The professor had a goatee and asked us
to consider whether we'd save a Rembrandt floating
out to sea, or the flailing disabled child with an IQ of fifty.
A long meditative silence swept through
the classroom. He paced with his hand on his chin,
in and out of September sunlight on that checkered floor.
At 19, I couldn't trust my voice,
which mostly hid in the depths of my throat
like a shivering creature on the brink of extinction.

He was just a respected philosopher
who'd taken up residence
in his own white head, supremely infected
with the residue of 20th century eugenics.
He had deep dark eyes and you could picture him
taking long walks and arguing with the ghost
of Immanuel Kant.

Another professor, also in love with neo-Darwinian
dilemmas, this man from Political Science, said
anyone who believes in altruism is willfully naïve.
I managed to raise my hand: *If we all agree*
altruism is impossible, we won't even try.
Doesn't the very idea let us off the hook?
He smiled and shook his head. *Wishful thinking,*
he said, and called on someone else.
As he turned his back I checked my face
in a pocket mirror. Was I ok?
He was so cute, and brilliant.

DIAGNOSIS

1.
I couldn't say the word dementia
for the first two years.
It seemed too cruel,
given her history of commitment
to hospitals whose job was to stun

her into silence, drug her dry-mouthed
down to earth, gift her with the Thorazine
shuffle, the Haldol hello, a look on her face
like a child under water, patiently drowning.

Always when I appeared that face broke through
the water, a blue-eyed sun, my momentary
mother, joyful and relieved to see a flash of home.

That's the face I carry
with me like a coin to toss
in the fountain of shame.

2.
Free will is mostly a cocktail
of myth and hope on the rocks.
"They made good choices" is not
an explanation — if I hear someone say it again
I might have to scream
have mercy on us all

as we hold onto reins
of bucking selves, gallop
over shadows laid down
beside the glowing bones of ancestors.

Does everyone feel accompanied
by someone who is not quite them,
hovering just outside the body,
afraid to come in?

When the hospital social worker
said dementia, hot waves rose in my chest
and refused to break, the flame
of *please no* in my face.
Softly, her manner stellar with kindness,
she told me my mother was brilliant,
the disease would probably move slowly:
"She should do lots of puzzles
and learn foreign languages."

3.
I joined my mother in the commons
room, where she dazzled her circle of friends
from the smoking court. I'd seen them
earlier, all exquisitely banished, huddled
in afternoon light, the black-eyed woman
with her stuffed bear, the tall young clown—
her favorite outcast of the day, the man
who wore three coats because she loved
that he wore three coats, and sang.

Of course, I wouldn't share the diagnosis
— not then, not ever —
this too would be a secret wall between us,
another one we'd scale
in wild moments, eye to eye,
on fire, indivisible.

UNCONTAINABLE

I didn't choose this rapture
that might never find its body.
It chose me, and I just kept
walking, and it followed me
the way the fingers of the blind
can follow a spine,
or a story they can't stop
reading, or like a trail of afternoon
sunlight follows itself into
evening.

Then he whispered
to me in a dream, "but don't you want
to be held in someone's arms,
naked, laughing by the window
in the middle of a winter
night?" I woke knowing
the absence of arms as absolute
presence was plenty
for now.

OLD MARY

They always show her as the young saintly woman who said Yes
when God wanted to impregnate her via the angel — so as to
tear open the heart of the world with light.

What I want to see now is not that beatific pale faced kid who
I sang to as a child, not that radiant gentle young beauty in her
blue veil, but the old woman she must have become, scorched by
sun, bitter winds, testing the patience of her friends with savage
grief, lines on her brown face rooted in sorrow and the grave.

I want Old Mary's veil to be made of fire. Her hands like claws.
Her eyes filled with knowledge of what this world can do — like
light from the moon that shines through broken windows in
these abandoned towns. Eyes that show how this world can take
what you love best and kill it.

Old Mary, full of grace, is the Lord still with thee? Blessed are
you among the breaking. Old Mary, barefoot in the sand, did
you sleep under a palm tree somewhere in Galilee? Did you
suffer insomnia, praying to stars?

Maybe you threw your head back to the moon. To think the
moon you knew is the moon I know. I know you missed him
until the day you died. Like any mother of any child. Someone
should paint you old, Mary.

"I'M IN LOVE WITH MY OWN THOUGHTS,"

says the monk
who can't fly
in his dreams anymore.
I especially like the thought
of my mother
in the light
of her small red kitchen,
sliding a glass of milk
across the table
to me,

this followed
by the thought
that I did not thank her
by the sea
when she gifted me
a bucket, shovel,
towel printed
with bluebirds.
I was old
before I learned anything
that matters.
This is the best
of my clutter.
I don't need
to burden you
with the worst.
I'll try again to offer that
to Silence.

SEVEN TEE-SHIRTS SPOTTED LAST NIGHT IN TARGET WHERE I
HAD TO GO GET A NEW CHARGER

1. I'M WITH STUPID (young sheet-white guy, alone, appeared to
have just emerged from a long hibernation, tee-shirt was tight.)

2. I'M THE NICEST ASSHOLE ON EARTH (heavy set Black woman
flanked by laughing friends, trailed by two little kids, letters on
the black tee-shirt were neon, wanted to follow them.)

3. OCEAN CITY, MARYLAND (tired white woman pushing
grandchildren who were absolutely silent, as if something had
recently stunned them, but one, maybe two years old, was busy
with his phone.)

4. BACK OFF MADAFAKAS (young nodding white guy with
headphones on)

5. PITT (probably the mother of a student whose tuition keeps
going up — she looked like she could star in an Excedrin
commercial.)

6. NOT MY PROBLEM (Black guy with white woman, holding
hands, and the woman in a long sleeveless dress and dramatic
dangling cat earrings.)

7. IS THIS HEAVEN? (Fortyish grey haired white man. I asked
him, do you get a lot of comments on your shirt? He looked
surprised and said, actually, nobody's ever said a word. As he
headed toward the escalator I called after him. "Pretty sure
this is heaven!" He didn't hear me. The ones who did hear me
looked very confused.

SAINT ROCCO PARADE

Saint Rocco rises
into blue August sky
on his elevated platform
with the dog who saved him,
the dog who brought him bread
when he was banished in a cave,
infected with the plague
he got from caring for the sick.
Rocco, a man who'd healed so many,
gave all he had to the poor, but couldn't heal
himself without his dog. The dog
who licked his terrible wounds clean.

To be a tourist — it's always painful —
and isn't it enough to be a tourist
in one's own country, one's own skin?
So why am I here trailing this strange
procession where fervent old women sing
in Italian *O Gran San Rocco Liberaci,*
some of them in the white lace veil I wore
at First Communion.

Presevare il mio corpo!

The Knights of Columbus are out in their feathery hats.
The old faithful tape dollar bills to the saint's wounded
leg, his tunic held up by his own marble hand.
An old man bows to kiss the dog's paws.
Crowds lined on porches stare, or wave.

The prayers, the hot sun, the crooked streets —
and whatever part of me still understands
the shreds of this faith leads me on.

Saint Rocco, patron saint of dogs, healer
of the sick and the dying, *Preservare il mio corpo.*
For I need time, time to understand
why I'm alive.

THE SEA LION WHO SAVED THE BOY WHO JUMPED FROM THE GOLDEN GATE

1.

All my slippery-slick dark life,
    whether at sea with a raft
        of sisters and brothers,
        or on rocks
    sprawled in a colony,
I've loved the water.

Sometimes
        in the depths
        I'll sleep,
then wake
to break
    through water's skin
        to look at stars —
        swallowing them with my eyes.

I've loved tunneling
        twisting
    turning
        celebrating
the impossible freedom
        of having no choice
        but to be who I am.

2.

When the boy came
falling
sinking
    he prayed from such
        depth
    his prayer changed

the water—
     turned on the lights in my cells.
I circled him underneath,
       bumping him upwards.
       again
       again
       and each time
       he found air
   his gasp
       was a rusted knife, rising
       from his throat.

I didn't know he'd come
     on a bus where
       he'd made
     a deal with himself:
if one other rider
     showed him kindness
       he wouldn't jump.

It was raining.
     The Coast Guard came
     on the boat with the headlight,
the two men saying
     Jesus Christ!
     it's a goddamn kid again!

And they pulled him up out of the water.

ELIAS, NEWBORN

How strange it seemed at first
for a giant soul to be crammed
into a tiny body.

But no, I had it wrong—
the tiny body was housed in the soul
and the soul shimmered
the blue of the room
as we lay together,
late August light
breathing in the window.

The soul tumbles
through the world
like a windstorm. The body's
a twig or a speck of dust on
the soul's long and undulating back.

Newborn Elias had the face of one
who understood sorrow
was an intricate part of the equation
that would not be solved on earth.
The light in those dark eyes searched
mine as if I could explain.

HUSHED

The little Carolina wren is singing in the pine tree.
The blossoming pear tree beside it bursts into applause.

Rain comes down, each drop landing like a star.
I try to catch those stars in my hands,

kissed today by a song of Mercy.
For a moment I forget all the names I call myself.

Five Postcards From Shame City, Siberia

1.
You'll be proud to hear I finally got a job
in Shame City, Siberia. They almost employed
me as a tour guide, but I didn't look good enough
in the hair shirt. What was I expecting? I spent
only nine rubles on that piece of crap. Didn't
think I'd be in this city so long, or would have
forked over ninety. I'm still friendly, and believe
I'd be a better tour guide than Boris, who thinks
he's so great, and really doesn't belong here.

2.
Never have I belonged anywhere like I belong
here. You might like to see me with my cheek
stuck to the frozen window on the train I take
to work each black morning, and how the snow
beyond the glass is illumined like an old lover's
back in a dream. I work in the foundry, where
those who go too far with feelings shovel
until their chests split open, so the sun's
white eye might penetrate straight through
the red tunnel of the heart. They say the Holy
Spirit is always trying to row a little boat there.

3.
I keep a tiny Buddha in my pocket.
Sometimes my hand dives in and holds on tight —
I'll start crying tears that tell me I love
being alive more than I know. In the foundry
my nickname's Chudak, Russian for Odd Duck,
and I don't even care. It's my birthright
to be here in Shame City, Siberia, where faces
grow hot trying not to remember.

4.

I've loved so many people, but it was always too
much, or too little. In Siberia I dream
I see my parents and apologize for leaving
the unwashed cups on the counter.
When I wake I hear their voices like the birds
who can't survive here, and wonder how much
a body can take before it becomes
a flock of birds, and scatters.

5.

Each night in the forest I sit on frozen needles,
humming prayers. I pour bowls of shame stew
straight down my gullet, burning myself raw
amid the white pine sisters. Then I suck the starred sky
into me like a train. I know if I ever see anyone
I know again, I'll be a different person,
chastened, restrained, maybe holding a small black dog
with a white collar, who will hear my confessions,
so I don't have to tell them
to you anymore.

SHE'S BECOMING A STAR

Her wheelchair is a throne.
I can feel a protective light
swirling around her. She shines
so that strangers
stop before us on these streets,
not even sure why they're drawn,
asking for blessings
from one who cannot bathe or dress
herself—she who when asked how she stays
happy in Assisted Living said,
"Blessed Mother Mary
does everything for me,"
she whose radiance is rooted in loss
of desire to critique the world.

TAKE MINDY

The way I get emails from people trying to sell me things! For instance: Daily I hear from someone named Mindy McHorse. I am not making that name up. Ms. McHorse wants to sell me writing tips and a magazine called *The Barefoot Writer*. The title meant to conjure what? Hemingway in Key West? I am no longer a person who buys magazines. Unless a snow storm is coming is and I'm missing mother, who loved her magazines. *Good Housekeeping, Redbook*—she was studying how to be normal. Mindy McHorse has shown up in my Inbox every day for four years. You start to wonder about people whose names ingratiate themselves into your consciousness. Take Mindy. Perhaps the oldest of the McHorse girls. When she was five she wanted nothing more than to save the world. She wore black boots. Felt a tiger slept in her heart. Had a firm handshake. A sideways smile. One night in the snow, I walked her to her house. The blue one at the end of the dirt road by the lake. Nobody was home. Where were all the McHorses? Why had they left no note? Oh but wait, they did leave a note! Dear Mindy, we have risen with our ascendant masters. You must stay on earth and feed the cat. Do not be afraid. Let silence be your teacher. Dine with your guardian angel. Someday you too will ascend. Love, Mom and Dad McHorse

II

By the Creek in Chatham a Tree Became a Room

Ancient willow branches rose up,
and spilled a green fountain
to the ground. On a windless day,

a day from childhood I can wear like a crown,
my hands grabbed hold to part them.
I stepped barefoot into that circular
room, made by the tree

that had been waiting forever to take me in,
to show me how to be
ravished, alone, in silence,

in crisp shade, down on my haunches,
shimmering walls of tiny leaves breathing
the illuminated borders of that secret getaway.

My small body filled with light
and deep green wings.

I Wanted to Be a Red Valley

Or a seed in a red valley, waiting.
Then I wanted you to know my name.
Then I wanted you to know
that wasn't my real name.

Can't you see? Can't you see me
under my name, waiting for you?

You on the street, unafraid to weep, you in the garden
telephoning the sky, you who walk in your bones
as if it's nothing special, you with the branches,
and you with the tail, you old ones stumbling on the curb.

And all of you who listen to Nina Simone
into the night—I wanted you
to help me burn every name
in the red valley, let the rain wash those ashes,
and feed the seed.

I wanted to tear off my face
and fling it to hang on a branch near other
masks in the blazing moon.

I wanted to be a tin can,
kicked by a bored child. Or the voice
in that can
singing help, like Nina Simone.

I wanted the child
to put the can to her ear
and feel another world calling,
and start to run.

I wanted to be you. To slip out of my
body once and for all and into yours,
or into several bodies,

a grand dispersal, the mad search for home.
I wanted to be like Nina Simone,
who had to visit hell,
but kept her saving voice,
and saves me still.

ROSEY, LEAVING

At eighteen, she sings

as if she's been alive for centuries — a voice
filled with old sorrow and violets,

the lost child on the twisted street,
the woman in a doorway with her hand on her brow
peering out in a season of drought.

And if her song rises,

you can hear the far-flung moon,
the man who turned his face away

and kept on walking. I could go on.
When she was five, she'd never heard opera

but woke up singing it.
I assumed her soul had traveled places

I couldn't see before she got to me,
and now she's leaving.

When she was six she wept with rage
when a wounded bird died in her hands.

I want to tell her there is no way
to thank her enough, that before she came
I was racing around a dark field,
looking for home.

Mothers are lovers and insane.
We think it will go on forever, and it will, but not like this,

ever again. This is the last day
she can walk through these rooms
and not be a visitor.

"ALL THE PRETTY LITTLE HORSES"

It was my favorite of the lullabies.
Dapples and greys, pintos and bays,
the little horses saved me
on the darkest days.

All the longing in that lullaby
could startle my infant into silence.
Nights falling asleep to the song
I'd see horses taking over
the house —

exhausted but ecstatic
to have that baby by my bed, a child
I would have died for again and again

to know the deep pleasure
of skin to skin — we had safety
and that song with the pretty little horses
as my child fell asleep knowing
those she loved were nearby, singing.

It would be twenty years before I'd learn
the beauty in the long ache
of melody and lyric was torn from a woman
with her own child, who she had to set down,

way down yonder, down in the meadow,
sweet little baby cryin' mama
the birds and the butterflies peckin' at his eyes
sweet little baby cryin' mama,

while up in the big house
she rocked another mother's child,
held to her breast,
his hungry white face.

By the time the song got to me,
they'd changed the words
"peckin'at his eyes"
to "fluttering nearby."

GRIEF IS A TIDE THAT'S GOING OUT

I can't stop writing letters
to the dead. I wish I was dropping
these endless missives to my father
into the mailbox up on the corner,
like a five year old believing heaven
has an earthly address.

If heaven has an earthly address, it must
be inside of the yes
of our no, the little windows
opening all around us that we can't see.

I know a man who was visited in a dream
by his late friend Larry who stood in a stream
quoting Theresa of Avila.

Maybe the dead write back
in the language of Sun. "Keep burning,
keep shining, be warm."

My friend Tanya from Russia
watched her dead grandfather eat pickled herring
in her Pittsburgh kitchen one night.
In his underwear he ate
with great relish, then cleaned up
the counter before his ghostly departure.

I've begged my father to come back
and have a drink, but he's
apparently not thirsty anymore.

Autumn Bus Ride

Steel gray shot through her dyed electric orange hair.
She wore the urgent sit-with-me face
I'd worn on darker days when I'd imagined a word or touch
from a stranger would be better than enduring
my own vast company,

which is a kind of faith in other people I didn't know I had then—
I'd called it desperation. And she had rigidly upright posture
like someone mocking the military
or off their meds, the last person I wanted to sit with,
so of course I slid right in —

she could have been my mother and Walt Whitman
reminds us to befriend the off-kilter
which at times meant befriending myself
but she was the more obvious case—the broken
lime green patent leather heeled sandals,
the brown nylons torn at the big toe,

and I tried staring out at the rain falling on people stranded
under newspaper hats, wet faces squinting alone
in Pittsburgh's gray evening as the bus sizzled
toward the red light seething exhaust.

Not done with men, are you? she said, nudging me.
I didn't answer, not because I didn't approve of this
as an opening question—it was the best
I'd heard in years. I just wanted to hear it enter the musty bus-air
one more time. Not done with men? and I said, No, you?

Every time I think I'm done, she said, a man walks by
and gets me here! She punched herself in the heart
and several riders turned. Then she laughed—not a real laugh
but a ha, ha, ha, with an accompanying loud clap.

My man's Tommy he blows litter off the sidewalk
up on Penn Avenue
with some kind of blowing machine called a blower.
I'm sixty one he's sixty and he got pictures of his house
in the Johnstown flood. I love him like a doll
and his middle name's Creek.
I said, does he love you back? And could
feel I'd ruined everything even before
she snapped *of course he does, why wouldn't he?*
We rode the rest of the way in silence, my face hot
with a curious grief.

Do you love? Then you're loved.
Hold that thought, all the way home.

I FORGET WHAT I CAME FOR

Oh, God, I don't want anyone to be distant!
—Hafez

I don't know if he spent as much time with angels
in taverns as he claims to in his poems,

but his words plant themselves behind the wall
in my heart, and open to a hidden sun.

I'm tired of ghosts in empty rooms, tired of strangers
in the massive store today, their faces hard
and determined, as if they too swallowed the lie
that everything depended on them.

In the aisles pushing my cart,
I forget what I came for, and leave
with items I don't understand,
like squash. I wish I could be on a good ship,

until loneliness passes, though Hafez
would say get sicker, get so lonely
the Great Physician of the soul must enter.

WHAT BINDS

He was in love
with the pain of changing
his mind

the verge
defining itself
when something he believed
cracked
and floated off

He spoke of how in the middle
of the day he'd suddenly crave
gray light
in a bare room
a cot with a tight blanket
by the window
snow falling in the wash stand mirror

to be far from words.
His eyes asked
what binds me
to this mass murdering

century, can you remind me
can you implicate me daily
my hands, my heart

can you take me to the ocean,
to the blue rooms with their corners
and their doorways
to my mother,
and my father
that place I ran from,
now I want it back.

Can you tell me how
to live without it,
to love the wrenching
song, the dirt,
these storms of anonymous
flowers spilled from the always
breaking open
heart of the Divine?

PINK DOOR

That was the day you walked
beside me for the last time.

Did I mention seeing
a pink door in the sky?

How it opened for the sun's face
and how the sun looked mighty

familiar that day? Like the eye of light
had a message for us I'm still

trying to conjugate.
And I was like, you know, *you* are

about the strangest treasure this side
of Moon, Pennsylvania. And you were like

Personally I feel like a map
torn to pieces in a hedgehog trap.

And I was like okay but what about
those pajamas you promised me?

And you were like I thought you said
pajamas reminded you of death.

And I was like everything reminds me
of death, and you were like

So sing about it, girl!
And then we linked arms on Cordova Street

where the elf house stands, and I was like
Okay, so we'll get divorced if you insist,

but next life we are living in the elf house.
And you were like Okay, deal.

Let Something Like a Tiny Sun

I never let myself think at a wedding—
I prefer to cry. It's beautiful and it hurts
to know you can't get married
even when you marry.

I walk out of the hall to look over the balcony--
wind in my face and
(I never let myself think at a wedding—
I prefer to cry) it's beautiful and it hurts
so I float right out of my body
on the wheeling wings
of other people's joy and desire.

Or feel encased, and like alarms
are sounding behind my face.
I wander, then discover
 a maroon velvet chair,
the kind you find in an elegant restroom
when you are drunk, confronting yourself
in the mirror exactly as you would
a stranger – hello there.

Then later, in the dark, I ask the stars,
Have the two dear ones begun to name
their damages?

(I never cry after a wedding,
but I can't help but think)
please don't let fear stalk the marriage
like a starved creature
hiding in the closet with a gun.

Let something like a tiny sun
rise between them on the coldest nights
of rattling tears.
Give them years and let grief enter
as it will when love arrives
to tear us open, or apart.

BOOTS

The moon's door finally swings open
a year after my mother dies.

I thought maybe piles of bones would fall out,
not this waterfall of milky light.

In a parking lot,
I write *thanks* on the dusty window
of a car.

I close my eyes and see the moon's
white light filling red rubber boots
I wore when I was five. Look,
they're out there muddy on the back stoop.
They took me up and down the streets
and through the rain and snow

in the long days when I knew
the ones I loved would live forever.

In the Galaxy Diner

I'd like one order of the Outrage with Courage, please,
with my usual side of slightly burned Purity of Intention.
I want to sit here all night in this empty booth
until the Holy Spirit tells me to slide over, make room.

I want the waitress to have just fallen in love
with Dusk framed in the window,
the ruffled clouds in red sky with orange flames
shooting out of the sun's sinking head.

I want the black wet parking lot
to lead to the rollicking green ocean,
the lace in the waves shining as they rise.
I want to talk to Saint Rocco who was saved
from the plague by a dog.

Or I just want coffee, strong and black,
rice pudding in a small bowl, Stevie Wonder's
My Cherie Amour on the juke.

Took No Distance

Patrick ushered me
through spitting rain
in London, late November.

Under a black awning
we burned our mouths on Turkish coffee
in tiny red cups.
Silence had us deep in its cave.

"Delicious," he said, the word
hovering in the wet gray air
before us like a flapping bird.

Hundreds marched with purpose
down the sidewalk
as if they'd never heard of death.

Something behind the bones in his face
kept opening like a bloom
of kindness every time he looked at me,

though my foundation
had crumbled, my poor father
dead without anything between us

settled. I grieved like a child.
He took no distance,

lost no patience.
Bought me a massage
from a gifted Chinese woman

in a cold, well-lit basement
where a metal table, sink,
and single light bulb made the room
bright even when I closed my eyes
and saw my father's face.

CAGED

So Jed tells me in the coffee shop
his friend wrote a play about love.
In it the husband begins turning
into a rabbit.

Little by little he acquires
a twitching nose, a soft coat,
beady reddish eyes, pauses
between hops that always come
as a terrible surprise.

At the end of the play
the husband's small, genuine in his cage.
The rabbit's wife is sitting
spot-lit in her chair, loving her husband
and his long, silken ears, counting
her blessings and saying sleepy
prayers, wondering if his cage
needs to be cleaned again today,
and if he's out of water.

And when will she get the knife out?
How will she flay and consume and digest
the great love of her life?

Assisted Living

I ask her
to imagine

she's on a ship

her childhood friends
dancing on the deck

all of them
under a soft
pink sky

Her eyes
light up
as the ship
heads out to sea

and she grabs
my hands

BLUE BLACK CUP

That blue black cup
sits empty on the sill.
I might give it a single green
marble, or a yellow leaf,
or a round white pill.
I might give it some old
pennies — or maybe
a shiny new one that would sit
like an eye on the cup's
bottom winking. Or I could
give that blue black cup
a little shard
of one of my best breaking
hearts, and some water.
I might just sit here
and think how beautifully
that cup receives all it's given.
I might be a student
of the cup, devoted to learning
how to receive this world.
How to stop making myself
shields of not now, no, no
thank you. As if time
is on my side and I can taste
and see the goodness
of the world later.

III

To Walk With Alyosha

To walk with Alyosha was one thing I wanted that year.
I glanced up from the snow in The Brothers Karamozov— a
book I couldn't read today, my phone having destroyed my
mind—and I smiled. Smiled and watched the snow   because I
was alive with Alyosha in January.

No. I was in love with Alyosha and I glowed. I was turning
twenty and immortal. Reading then was like falling into a
sacred well of echoes. At the bottom of the well I'd look up and
see a little glimpse of heaven. I can't return to Alyosha and that
time before the phone destroyed my mind

but I can remember how purple roads below me in the dusk led
to an infinity that seemed to be hiding inside of future moments.
I can conjure the black dawn, turning on the green lamp,
diving back into the book, and finding him there, in that attic of
the old house filled

with soft orange light, my blanketed bed tucked into the alcove
in the sky. I was used to being torn to pieces then; you can't be
whole when yearning is always taking you so far out of your
body. Even the pine tree at the window was a hook. But my
heart fell perfectly into the book, with Alyosha.

His soul was like a smooth black sun-struck stone on a sill, a
stone I wanted to put in my mouth, like his name. Purity of
soul like a whole country governed by a single daffodil. The sun
was the face behind his own face. Sometimes I thought Alyosha
was all I needed.   And yet it's true that with him by my side, I
carried a measuring stick and used it to beat myself. Is that what
everyone did?

I'd see him breathing beside me like Jesus in a black coat by the
Volga River. So close he could hear my whispers. He'd talk of
angels, relief from pain.

How in his vast heart's dream there was "the secret renewal for all, that all will love one another. And there will be neither rich nor poor, neither exalted nor humiliated."

And so I would clutch his hand and work hard to drink his innocence. I would find some words to display the shape of my loneliness. I would make him borsht and do somersaults while quoting the Gnostics. Strange to believe we have to work so hard to be loved. Even by a fictional character.

GO AHEAD, ROAR

Frank Johnson from the Pittsburgh zoo
calls, says he reviewed my application
and would like to give me a phone interview
the year I was living on noodles
with no air conditioner in record breaking heat
trying to believe in myself as a writer.

Frank Johnson says First, can you roar like a lion
and I say Excuse me, and he says, I know
it sounds odd but we want to hire people who have a heart
for animals, and the best way to measure this
is listening to people roar. It gives us a good
indication of—

Seriously?

So, would you like to give it a shot?
I go to the window
to find a stranger in the street
who might look up and see me mouthing
"What the fuck?"

But the hot street is empty.
Frank says, You'll be working with children,
as if I'd understand, which I do.

The interview is strange,
but not as bad as the one I'd had with the boss who'd asked me
to pretend I was on a catwalk and sat spying
over the top of his *Conan The Barbarian* comic book
as I carried a tray on my shoulder up and down
the aisle of the restaurant several times,
while he scanned me, then hired me
only to fire me two weeks later saying
something about you just isn't right.

I'm down to sixty bucks.

I roar and roar and roar
myself straight into the heart of the lion
as if I'll never need to come back out again.

Someplace Wild

I think of all these feelings as children.
I don't want them driving the car,
but I also don't want them locked in the trunk.

I buckle them in, drive them
to someplace wild in the night.

All right, out of the car!

They charge the dark field. I head up a tree.
I cheer them on from on high, seeing
they have little to do with me.

Instead I'm making friends with night birds,
and this surprising old, bald doll someone left
in the crotch of these branches. Her battered face
shines in my hands like a fallen moon.

LITTLE ESSAY ON A FRIEND

I remember him suggesting I use the exclamation point
a little less when we corresponded. This made me laugh
until I almost cried—I can't explain why. Maybe I liked
being trusted not to take offense. He had other critiques of me—
I was "too nice" and why would I ever buy students pizza?
What was I thinking? Students should buy *me* pizza!

And later, when he was dying: Why did I presume I knew
him well enough to tell someone else how he was doing?
That last one hurt. He could sting. But I didn't mind being
stung. He lived always at the absolute mercy of himself
while I curated, contained, rearranged myself,
presented what I hoped was the best version. You'd think
I'd get tired of that, you'd think I would have learned to mirror

his wild, unedited honesty, but no. And yet
before he knew he was dying, there were long days
when life seemed as bright as an orange on a tree in the fog,
hanging on a reachable branch, dangling before my eyes
so that sometimes my whole mind filled with orange.
Like I was carrying around the sun, carrying it up and down
the blue steps in the library, the mossy green steps
of the ruined church, the black steps in my mind that ended
midway up because I was so often suspended,
not knowing where I was.

Once he said he wished he was a fly on the wall
of my unimaginable life. Like, why were so many strangers
in my house? Why did I not sleep at night? Who really mattered,
and how? It had been so long since anyone felt such burning curiosity.
Years and years. I'd been living with those who saw me
as solved, when I felt so unsolvable.

Irascible friend, send me a ghost email saying
You should really wear better shoes.
Or *Count your breaths before they're gone.*

THIS WORLD WANTS YOU EVERY DAY

Trees just stand there, waiting, always ready
to greet you without rebuke
for all the days you walk by as if they're nothing,
as if they're not standing there
giving and giving and giving.

When my father died and my family fell
apart, I dreamed I was adopted
by the Douglas-Firs. In the middle
of the shaded grove, I saw an old wooden desk

and took my seat. Was I back in school?
Where were the kids and the teacher? Maybe
it was too late to learn, and I'd have to sit here,
hands folded forever?

Then all the trees lifted their branches
in the wind together.

As Long As I Can Be Everyone

> "We yearn for our original light."
> — Jeannine Marie Pitas

Here in this mountain town in Italy, I want to be that old man
for a while, the one on the dance floor in this public square,
stomping out his story in black Italian shoes as the band blasts
80's music under sharp, Italian stars after we've stepped out
of a large tent where I sat with people at long tables eating
too much cheese and buttered pasta. We all exploded

when Tammy said the odd salad is a little too much like lawn.
I want to be Tammy, and also James, unable to dance, missing
his Los Angeles lover. I want to be James loving Lenny that much
or be the twirling girl who read our Animal Spirit cards the night
before, telling me I leave parties early because I'm shadowed by Fox.

She believes animal spirits will not let her become someone
she's not meant to be. When I'm finished being her,
I'll be the teacher-playwright known for plays about genocides.
I could cross my arms and be his handsome, bald, shy, self
who plans next year to walk the way Saint Francis made alone

in the Umbrian mountains, but now he is saying no to the twirler
when she asks him to dance, and I watch her beautiful
Egyptian face stay open even in this rejection.
Sign me up to be her, confident, stormy, a theater teacher
in Hong Kong, marrying for the first time when she's home
from this Italian escapade, this luxury I couldn't have imagined
would be part of my life. I'd also like to be the Italian women
watching at the tables—old, finally settled in their bodies, laughing
together, sipping wine, only sometimes allowing the men
to take their hands, pull them to the floor,

except for one who's been dancing with her husband all night,
the two of them like twins, short as children, cheek to cheek
with their eyes closed. I can't bear that sweetness now.
Let me be the cool, observant rising moon.
What did Kierkegaard say about not wanting to be the self?

Was that *The Sickness Unto Death*? I forget nearly everything
he wrote, but not the love I felt when his electric sorrow
opened a door in the universe I could walk through. I
don't mind being myself, as long as I can be everyone else, too.

SEARCHED

I saw him at a small party,
his diagnosis sitting beside him on the couch

like a leashed creature nobody would touch
or name.

He leaned toward others as they spoke—his interest
in their lives a willed presence in that room,

his eyes radiant with isolation
as they searched us,

his face, stained yellow like a child's hands
after a long day with dandelions.

Rooting for You

I'm gonna put you in a book,
give you a little blue house by a creek,
a clown-fish, and a parakeet,
child-feet charging
over prickles and pebbles so you can
meet the dog-minister on the other side.

Nothing in this world
like a sermon from a dog,
a dog in the sun in cool October.
It's all about breath
and running without destination—
that's part of giving you a beautiful
brambly childhood, and if you're willing
to take it, I could also put glow in the dark stars
on your ceiling, sober up your parents,
give you ice skates for the city,
two best friends who take your hands
and threaten to kill the ones who call you slut.
You'll throw your head back and laugh
in the next long chapter by the sea.
I'll make sure you comprehend the sky
is always rooting for you.

Because each story needs a little
something tragic,
you'll barely survive a car accident
and fall in love with the paramedic
who tells you you're going to be just fine,
bandaging you while singing, as you learn
you're the type who needs to get badly hurt
before you can feel you deserve
the glass of water, the hand, the song.

The paramedic's mother who looks like Cher
will take the three of you to Santa Monica
for no reason. You'll win a juggling contest
in Minneapolis on your fortieth birthday.
You and your kid will know how to open
your mouths to the rain.

I'm working on the structure of the thing.
Loving you more than you know.

Hog Days, or The Magic of Capital Letters

Forget how all day long you felt
like a big hog who knew nothing.

Become instead,
The Hog Who Knew Nothing.

Smiling Hog is filled with mischief,
singing hog-songs, kissing dead flowers,

flopping into puddles of mud before
following some kid home.

Of course the kid can't invite the hog in,
so Hog wanders off alone.

But can't you see that orange sun?
The dancing lights in windy yellow reeds?

And look, the hog angel
makes her appearance

for the first time on earth, in the pages
of this book, following the hog forever, the end.

UKRAINE

In Kyiv, home to my long dead grandfather,
the war is beginning, and here in Pittsburgh
we're watching it on tv—the camera swooping
across the endless lines of those escaping—
people stalled in cars trying to get to Poland,
people at bank machines cleaning out money,
people waiting in grocery stores to stuff backpacks.
And the longest line by far, says the reporter,
his camera letting us see,
are the people lined up in the cold to give blood.

SKULLS ON THE TABLE

To all the disappearing ones:
I miss you, I hope
you're in the sun

or in a moon-bath,
or in the far corner of a dream
running through a sprinkler in the stars,
wondering who you are, who you
were, who you might be when the scars
lift like a flock of red birds.

I am sorting socks and humming
on the bottom step
on New Year's Eve,
resolving to make stained
glass windows in the coming
year, if only in my mind.

I read once of a monastery
where they arranged
skulls on the table to remind all
of our shared destination

and one young monk named Jinpa
put roses in the eye-sockets,
"because a skull can be a vase, baby."

Never Coming Again

The day I broke out of the life sentences
encircling my dear thorax
was the day I knew the insides of my calves
could easily be turning green
with unsalvageable vines.

If this is not a way to say "Scared of dying,"
speak to me. Remind me you are never
coming near again.

Last night counting moon coins, huddled
in a torn black field, I prayed the children
we never had would be named for inviolable
saints, like Dot in the cafeteria,
who wept when the heavy girl said:
"No cake today, M'am, my cat died last week."

I followed that girl.
I needed to learn to love a cat too much.

When I was small, I cut a worm in half,
and still sometimes wonder if that divided creature
ever found itself conjoining.

If it was a planarian flatworm, it had a chance.
Planarians re-grow lost heads, memories intact.

So I will be your miracle-namer in the distance.
Miracle of 60 thousand miles of blood vessels
inside our bodies.

Crouched down in a rainy gutter with pebbles glistening,
I'm dreaming you might see me.

What I want is for you to hear my breathing,
like the child you were, holding the seashell to your ear
one evening, when all the others had departed
and you knew that little fire of solitude—
that little fire of solitude by the sea.

The Giant

My beautiful giant
friend was really alive once,

living up on Callowhill in Pittsburgh,
the apartment unfurnished
except for a couch.

We had spaghetti and butter breakfasts at dawn.
We'd both been placed into divorce-
dumpsters, lids slammed shut.

The laughter of childhood
returned to our bodies
like rain. He could read my mind.

If he saw me on the street, he'd imitate
the preacher we'd heard on an old cassette:

Hey! You doin' your love-walk out here?
You gotta do your love-walk now!
Come on!

HIDDEN

If I could only explain how red it is
here in July. How the tomatoes
contain hearts that beg
to be broken open.
How the moon blushes
as if ashamed
to be so long suspended
alone in darkness.
And on the television
not a single coffin of a soldier
will be seen.
But we'll hear a story
told by a sunburned neighbor
we barely know
about a boy who never
made it back
from his second tour.
How his fiery wife
took to sleeping
on park benches after that.
Screamed at strangers.
How everyone said she had never
been quite right in the head—
it wasn't that the war
blowing her husband to pieces
changed her.

SARAH ELIZABETH ADAMS

Sarah Elizabeth Adams, called Sallie,
was five years old when her mother was sold.

The slave dealer lived in Lynchburg.

Sallie herself was sold that same day,
but not with her mother,
not with her mother.

Thomas Thurman purchased Sallie
to care for his ailing wife,
and let me repeat, Sallie was five.

She would never see her mother again.
Never would she ever see her mother again.

She would live to tell the story
of how she'd sometimes slip
away from the sick woman

to search for solace under a tall white-oak.
She'd wrap her arms
around the tree's wide trunk,
and cry.

Even if she was
the only child ever sold,
the only one torn from the arms
of a tremulous mother,

such sorrow would be enough
to break the humiliated heart
of the earth

a million times over.

"GO SCREW YOURSELF"

Today I opened Hafez to a poem called "Go Screw Yourself."
People used to say this, before *Go Fuck Yourself* gained favor.
"Screw" seems old-fashioned, like maybe you'd say it,
a deeply offended secretary, to a man in a fedora
on a cold night before you walk away.

Or maybe a grade-school principal having a nervous
breakdown would say it on the intercom one day.
It would go down in the school's history of hysterics
and the man would be fired, but he was the one
who cared, who thought his teachers working without
supplies in that ravaged school where doors were torn
off lavatory stalls and children came to school hungry,
were *heroes*. He's probably still dreaming of them.

When everything is breaking down, shouldn't a person
be a mirror for a moment, so we can see the truth?
Would Hafez say no? By the way he is not saying
Go Screw Yourself to people, but to illusions that knock
with fists at the door, lies that ring the bell
and beg us to come out to chase them down the street
against the traffic, like dogs after slabs of flying meat.

I never want to follow the illusion that hating someone
can get me somewhere. But I am so tired of these little
hung juries of the heart, these stupefied judges,
these long, tattered cords of compassion.

WHY I'M SINGING

Because snow filled the shoes I left on the porch,
I woke up and found them, and wished I could tell you.

Because I need you to keep me tethered to here,
to let each breath steer me toward the light of the next.

Because all the ships are leaving the black, starlit harbor,
And ghosts on deck are still believing in us.

Because singing on the darkened road will lead to crying,
and there's a chemical in tears known to be medicinal.

Because animals sing, and they're our sages.
Because Sky.

Because Leslie said, "There's no upside to despair. Do
something."

Because melted snow rivers these roads
where light from the sun is skipping like a stone.

TODAY'S REQUESTS

Transmute my rage

at the gun lovers

if only for today.

Turn me into silk

like the voice

of Marvin Gaye.

Let me gather

by a bonfire,

and hold stones.

Remind me to use

all my measuring sticks

for kindling.

A Partial Catalogue

Brother says he's growing tomatoes inside,
other brother's selling tee-shirts by the seashore.
Father is often walking beside me in spirit
even if I'm sure I never loved him well enough.
A friend sits on a swing like a member of today's
paradise and I only envy her beauty a little.
Discussed why the urge to articulate the self
in long sculpted letters dies down with age.
Other friend phoned, recalled we were once
thirteen dying of laughter in Burger King.
Little dog beside me licks her nose
with grace. I forgot to mention waking
with a smile. What had I been dreaming?
Saw a friend's bearded husband emanating
joy talking of Joy Division. Decided
I won't regret not giving Izzie the Voracious
more chocolate. Mother sings *You'll Never Know*
on Face Time from Assisted Living.
Made yet another vow to appreciate
even my wrong moves and decided
to call them exquisite.
Promised myself to take food
to Mercedes who lost her mother to the virus.
Prayed several prayers
for Marie in Saint Louis,
who's suffering after a still-birth.
Walked with Denson the ex-paratrooper
who reminded me there's no such thing
as bad weather. Created in my mind a bumper sticker
that said Yahweh or The Highway!
Texted my cousin Scott to see if he thought
that pun could make me rich.
Ate yogurt with frozen blueberries.
Good but not as good as double

chocolate Razzy Fresh which everyone needs
to try. Got email with subject line:
Mattress of Death. Oh, and that red iced tea!
And the guy who fixed our gas-line,
And Lydia the neighbor waving
with her toddler Nina the Dynamo
chalking up the sidewalk.
Decided in a resolute way that my fear
I'm never going to feel at home
on earth can also be called exquisite.
Ordered take out Thai food.
Looked forward to watching a documentary
about seeing eye dogs. Wrote this partial
catalogue of August the 7th, a day when
I imagined nothing much happened.

ACKNOWLEDGEMENTS

My deepest thanks to editor Ruth Thompson, and designer Don Mitchell of Saddle Road press for their expertise and labor of love.

And also to the following poet-friends for reading for me, and offering community and inspiration: Janet Arida, Tony Hoagland, Nancy Krygowski, Rick St. John, Dani Leone, Laurie McMillan, Ellen McGrath Smith, Emily Mohn-Slate, Philip Terman, and Lawrence Wray.

Special thanks to Nancy Krygowski for convincing me to make this book, and for all her generous expertise along the way. And to Lawrence Wray, the most careful and insightful of copy-editors. Philip Terman also offered helpful suggestions for edits of the manuscript.

Thank you to colleagues and students, past and present, to poet and long-time pen-pal, Jim Schley, who's gifted me with books of poems for decades, to Charlotte Daniels for listening to my earliest attempts and cheering me on, to my family, especially Patrick, Rosemary and Elias, and to enduring all-weather friends.

Thank you also to my centering prayer group, for all our years together.

"Take Mindy" is for Dani Leone, editor of Tiny Day.
"Go Ahead, Roar" is for Bob Finegan.
"Hushed" is for Mary White.

Thanks to the editors of the following journals:

Soul Lit who published "Grief is a Tide That's Going out" and "Old Mary" and "She's Becoming a Star"

Healing Muse who published "Searched"

Chatauqua Review who published *"Bolivian Orphanage" and "I Wanted to be A Red Valley"*

Pittsburgh Poetry Review who published "Autumn Bus Ride" and "Go Ahead, Roar"

Pittsburgh Post Gazette who published "Do You Speak Hafez?"

Café Review who published "Partial Catalogue," "Tree Shadows," and "Never Coming Near Again"

The Windover who published "Uncontainable"

Presence who published "What Binds" and "In the Galaxy Diner"

Literary Mama who published "Rosey, Leaving"

Several of these poems have appeared in a Newman chapbook, *Moon's Door.*

About the Author

Jane McCafferty is author of two story collections and two novels. Her work has received an NEA, two Pushcarts, the Drue Heinz prize, and other awards. She writes poetry, fiction, and non-fiction, and publishes in a variety of literary journals. She is grateful to be teaching at Carnegie Mellon, and for Madwomen in the Attic at Carlow.

www.ingramcontent.com/pod-product-compliance
Lightning Source LLC
Chambersburg PA
CBHW030502130626
46549CB00007B/2821